STARS OF SPORTS

# FERNANDO TATÍS JR.

## BIG-TIME HITTER

■■▮ by Matt Chandler

CAPSTONE PRESS
a capstone imprint

Published by Capstone Press, an imprint of Capstone
1710 Roe Crest Drive, North Mankato, Minnesota 56003
capstonepub.com

Library of Congress Cataloging-in-Publication Data
Names: Chandler, Matt, author. Title: Fernando Tatis Jr. : big-time hitter / By Matt Chandler.
Description: North Mankato, Minnesota : Capstone Press, an imprint of Capstone, [2022] | Series: Sports Illustrated Kids stars of sports | Includes bibliographical references and index. | Audience: Ages 8-11 | Audience: Grades 4-6 | Summary: "Baseball runs in the family for Fernando Tatis Jr. Both his father and grandfather played professional baseball. Tatis signed his first professional baseball contract when he was just 16 years old! He made his major league debut a few years later and broke an age record that same day. Learn more about this Dominican shortstop superstar!"— Provided by publisher.
Identifiers: LCCN 2021028247 (print) | LCCN 2021028248 (ebook) | ISBN 9781663983589 (hardcover) | ISBN 9781666323221 (paperback) | ISBN 9781666323238 (pdf) | ISBN 9781666323252 (kindle edition)
Subjects: LCSH: Tatis, Fernando, Jr., 1999—Juvenile literature. | Baseball players—United States—Biography—Juvenile literature. | Baseball players—Dominican Republic—Biography—Juvenile literature.
Classification: LCC GV865.T27 C43 2022 (print) | LCC GV865.T27 (ebook) | DDC 796.357092 [B]—dc23 LC record available at https://lccn.loc.gov/2021028247 LC ebook record available at https://lccn.loc.gov/2021028248

Editorial Credits
Editor: Christianne Jones; Designer: Bobbie Nuytten; Media Researcher: Morgan Walters; Production Specialist: Laura Manthe

Image Credits
Associated Press: Andrew Woolley, 15, Gregory Bull, 5, 18, Jeff Chiu, 24, Kathy Willens, 9, Kiyoshi Mio/Icon Sportswire, 23, Mark Goldman/Icon Sportswire, 21; Getty Images: Andria Patino, 13; Newscom: Brian Rothmuller/Icon Sportswire DHZ, Cover, Jon Endow/Image of Sport, 28, K.C. Alfred/TNS, 27; Shutterstock Premier: Alberto Calvo/EPA-EFE, 17; Shutterstock: Eugene Onischenko, 1, sa2ukedr, 11; Sports Illustrated: Nils Nilsen, 7

Source Notes
Page 8, "I remember my dad…" Bernie Wilson, "Padres phenom Tatis Jr. born to play in the big leagues," Atlantic Journal-Constitution, March 5, 2018, https://www.ajc.com, Accessed July 14, 2021.
Page 8, "I was already there…" Bernie Wilson, "Padres phenom Tatis Jr. born to play in the big leagues," Atlantic Journal-Constitution, March 5, 2018, https://www.ajc.com, Accessed July 14, 2021.
Page 12, "the Dominican Derek Jeter…" ESPN, "Bringing joy back to Baseball," Go Dominican Republic, August 10, 2020, https://www.godominicanrepublic.com, Accessed July 14, 2021.
Page 23, "unwritten rules…" Chuck Schilken, "Fernando Tatis Jr.'s grand slam vs. MLB unwritten rules: Whose side are you on?" Los Angeles Times, August 18, 2020, https://www.latimes.com, Accessed July 14, 2021.
Page 27, "Statue contract…" Associated Press, "Fernando Tatis Jr. cites legacy as reason for 14-year deal with San Diego Padres," Entertainment and Sports Programming Network, February 22, 2021, https://www.espn.com, Accessed July 14, 2021.

All internet sites appearing in back matter were available and accurate when this book was sent to press.

# TABLE OF CONTENTS

Words in **BOLD** are in the glossary.

# RECORD BREAKER

San Diego Padres rookie shortstop Fernando Tatís Jr. walked to the plate. More than 44,000 Padres fans cheered wildly. It was March 28, 2019, and Tatís was making his major league **debut**. The Padres were hosting the San Francisco Giants on Opening Day.

Tatís stepped into the batter's box. On the mound was All-Star pitcher Madison Bumgarner. Tatís worked the count to two balls and one strike. Bumgarner delivered his fourth pitch and Tatís swung hard. He ripped the ball past diving Giants third baseman Evan Longoria. Tatís delivered a huge hit in his first major league at bat!

He finished the game with a second hit as the Padres beat the Giants 2–0. Tatís became the youngest player to have a multi-hit game on Opening Day since Milwaukee Brewers player Robin Yount did it in 1975.

>>> Fernando Tatís Jr. celebrates his winning debut for the San Diego Padres on March 28, 2019.

# CHAPTER ONE

# BORN TO BE A BALLPLAYER

Fernando Tatís Jr. was born on January 2, 1999, in San Pedro de Macoris, Dominican Republic. At that time, his father, Fernando Tatís Sr., was in the major leagues with the St. Louis Cardinals. Tatís was literally born into the game of baseball. When Tatís's dad was in the United States playing ball, he was being raised by his mother, Maria. Tatís is the oldest of five children. He grew up close to his brothers Joshua, Elijah, and Daniel, and his sister, Maria.

More than 40 percent of families live in poverty in the Dominican Republic. But Tatís was raised in a resort town near the beach. His dad's success in baseball set Tatís up to follow in his footsteps. Tatís grew up in a household where the two most important things were family and baseball.

>>> Fernando Tatís Jr. with his dad, Fernando Tatís Sr., at a Major League Baseball event

# FOLLOWING IN HIS DAD'S FOOTSTEPS

Outside of the U.S., the Dominican Republic produces more major league players than any country in the world. Tatís is one of four members of his family to play pro ball. His dad played for five different teams over 11 years in the majors. His grandfather played in the Houston Astros organization. In 2019, his brother Elijah signed with the Chicago White Sox.

But it was his dad that inspired Tatís as a boy. "I remember my dad was taking me to the field. It was fun. It was great," Tatís said in a 2018 interview. "It was a thing that I love and that was the first love that I brought to this game."

"I was already there playing for the Cardinals," Tatís's dad said. "As soon as he opened his eyes, everything he watched was big league baseball."

>>> Fernando Tatís Sr. slams a hit with the New York Mets in 1999.

## FACT

Tatís's dad is the only player in major league history to hit two **grand slams** in one inning. He set the record on April 23, 1999, in a game against the Los Angeles Dodgers. Coincidentally, Fernando Tatís Jr. also homered twice in a game on April 23, 2021, against the Dodgers!

# CHAPTER TWO
# DOMINICAN BALL

For many boys growing up in the Dominican Republic, baseball is the center of their lives. They play ball from a very early age. Many live in poverty. They see baseball as their best chance to earn money, help their families, and build a bright future.

As boys get older, they are divided up. The best **prospects** leave their families to live with a baseball trainer. They all have the same goal: to earn a spot in a Major League Baseball academy. Each major league team runs an academy to train the next generation of ballplayers.

Tatís was in a much better position. Because of his dad's career, his family had money. He didn't have to quit school. He didn't have to leave his family to train.

>>> A baseball field in the
Dominican Republic

# GETTING HIS SHOT

By the time he was 14, Tatís had been training for more than half his life to play baseball. Scouts began to take notice. Sons of major league players often get extra attention. They grow up around the ballpark and spend a lot of time with professional players. Tatís is one example of that exposure paying off.

In 2013, a scout watching Tatís work out asked him what he wanted to be when he grew up. The teenager replied, "The Dominican Derek Jeter." Even then, he saw a huge future for himself in baseball. He believed in himself and his talent.

But there were many talented international ballplayers at that time. Future stars Vladimir Guerrero Jr. and Juan Soto were both ranked above Tatís on the top 30 International Prospects List. He didn't let that stop him.

〉〉〉 A teenage Tatís plays baseball in the Dominican Republic.

## Teen Star

It is fairly common for teenagers in the Dominican Republic to sign professional baseball contracts. The rules allow teams to sign players once they turn 16. Still, most of them take years to make it to the major leagues. Many never make it. Not Tatís. He signed his first pro contract when he was 16. He was playing professionally for the Padres by the time he was 17.

# CHAPTER THREE

# MINOR LEAGUE TIME

Tatís was a teenage prospect playing baseball in the Dominican Republic in 2015. Then the Chicago White Sox called. The Sox signed Tatís to his first professional baseball contract in July 2015. The team paid him a $700,000 **signing bonus**.

Tatís never played for the White Sox. The team traded him to the San Diego Padres in 2016. He was sent to the Padres rookie-league team in Arizona. Tatís began the season playing Class-A ball for the Fort Wayne TinCaps in April 2017. Tatís crushed 21 home runs and stole 29 bases for the TinCaps. In late August, he was promoted to the Double-A San Antonio Missions.

After a strong 2018 season in Double-A ball in San Antonio, Tatís ranked as the top prospect in baseball. He was ready for the major leagues!

>>> Tatís bats for the Fort Wayne TinCaps in the spring of 2017.

**FACT**

Tatís's $700,000 signing bonus was almost 20 times what the average worker in the Dominican Republic earns in an entire year!

# WINTER BALL

During the baseball off-season, many minor league players participate in the winter leagues. These are professional leagues in warmer places like Puerto Rico, Mexico, and the Dominican Republic.

The Padres allowed Tatís to play in the Dominican Winter League for two years after they signed him. Because he was so young, his time playing winter ball gave him great experience. He also got to play in his home country of the Dominican Republic. Tatís even played on Estrellas Orientales, a team managed by his dad! Estrellas Orientales won the championship during the 2018–2019 season—the same year both father and son were on the team.

**FACT**

Tatís returned to the Dominican league for the winter season in 2020 after two seasons as the starting shortstop for the Padres.

>>> Estrellas Orientales players congratulate each other after a victory.

>>> Tatís has had the opportunity to celebrate many home runs with his teammates since 2019.

# SUPERSTAR START

The Padres were at the end of spring training in 2019 when the announcement was made. After three seasons in the minors, Tatís earned a spot on the team's Opening Day roster!

On April 1, 2019, Tatís showed off his power. The Padres trailed the Arizona Diamondbacks 9–1 in the bottom of the sixth inning when Tatís stepped to the plate. He turned on the first pitch he saw from Merrill Kelly and drove the ball deep to left field. The crowd leaped to their feet. Tatís had hit his first major league home run!

One of his best games that year came on July 7 against the Dodgers. Tatís led off the game with a long home run to deep center field. In the fifth inning, he added a three-run homer. The Padres beat the Dodgers 5–3.

# INJURIES

In 2019 many baseball experts picked Tatís to be the National League (NL) Rookie of the Year before the season even began. He might have won the award, but he was unable to stay healthy. After getting off to a hot start, the rookie injured his hamstring in late April. He missed 34 games as he healed.

Tatís returned to the team on June 6 against the Washington Nationals. He picked up where he left off. He scored a run and showed his brilliance making plays at shortstop.

The Padres were still in the hunt for a **playoff** spot. Then Tatís was injured again. This time he hurt his back. The injury ended his rookie season. Even with missing 78 games, Tatís still finished his first year in the big leagues with 22 home runs and 53 runs batted in (RBIs).

>>> Tatís on the ground after injuring his hamstring on April 28, 2019.

## FACT

Although he missed almost half of the season, Tatís earned enough votes to finish third in the 2019 National League Rookie of the Year Award voting.

# CHAPTER FOUR

# PLAYING THROUGH THE PANDEMIC

2020 should have been Tatís's breakout year as he returned from his back injury. Instead, **COVID-19** delayed the start of the season until July. Once the season began, Tatís produced mixed results.

His biggest improvement was in his defense. In 2019, Tatís led all of baseball with 14 throwing errors out of a total of 18 errors. He promised to improve his defense in the off-season. He delivered on that promise. In 2020, Tatís committed just three errors in 57 games.

The biggest drop in his game in 2020 came at the plate. Tatís hit .317 in his rookie season. In 2020, he dropped 40 points in batting average, hitting just .277. Still, he crushed 17 home runs and helped lead the Padres to the playoffs. He even finished fourth in the National League Most Valuable Player voting.

## The Unwritten Rule

The Padres were leading 10–3 in the eighth inning of an August 17, 2020, game against the Texas Rangers. The bases were loaded. Rangers pitcher Juan Nicasio threw three straight balls to Tatís. He swung at the next pitch and crushed a grand slam home run. The Rangers were upset. They thought he shouldn't swing at a 3-0 pitch with such a big lead. It is one of baseball's "unwritten rules." Tatís was forced to apologize for hitting a grand slam!

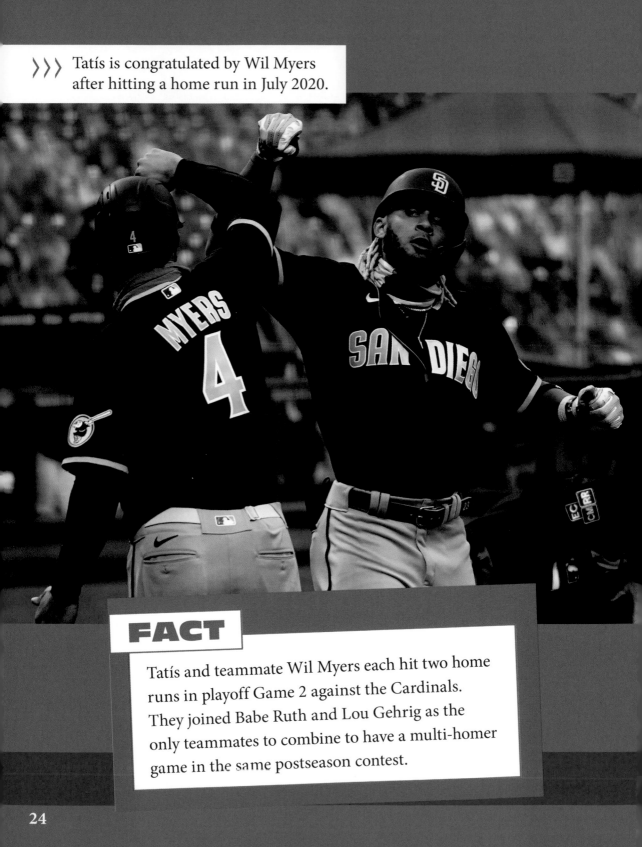

>>> Tatís is congratulated by Wil Myers after hitting a home run in July 2020.

**FACT**

Tatís and teammate Wil Myers each hit two home runs in playoff Game 2 against the Cardinals. They joined Babe Ruth and Lou Gehrig as the only teammates to combine to have a multi-homer game in the same postseason contest.

# PLAYOFF TIME

Tatís helped the Padres finish the 2020 season in second place in the National League West. Their record of 37–23 was good enough to earn a spot in the playoffs.

San Diego took on the Cardinals in the National League Wild Card round of the playoffs. The young slugger went 5-for-11 at the plate with two home runs. He also scored five runs and drove in five runs. His offense led the Padres to a two-games-to-one series win against the Cardinals.

The team advanced to play the Dodgers in the NL Division Series. Padres fans began to dream about their team returning to the World Series for the first time since 1998. But Tatís ran out of gas against the Dodgers. He had just two hits in 11 at bats with no runs driven in as the Dodgers **swept** the Padres three-games-to-none. The season for the Padres was over.

# CHAPTER FIVE

# A BRIGHT FUTURE

Tatís has already built a reputation as a fun-loving fan favorite. From social media to product endorsements, fans love to follow him and see what he is up to off the field. He is a young, famous, **elite** athlete.

In 2020, Tatís signed a deal to be a spokesperson for Gatorade. He is also paid to endorse Adidas and BMW. All of this adds up to millions of dollars in off-the-field earnings.

Tatís is also active on social media. He has more than 871,000 Instagram followers and 114,000 Twitter followers. Tatís is loved in San Diego, and he is also a national fan favorite. In 2020, more than 1,000 players played in the majors. Tatís was so popular he had the third best-selling jersey in baseball in 2021!

〉〉〉 Tatís signs autographs during spring training in 2020.

## Statue Contract

In February 2021, Tatís signed a new contract with the Padres. The deal was for 14 years and will pay him $340 million! The contract is the longest in the history of baseball. Tatís said his goal was to play his entire career in San Diego. The team called the deal a "statue contract." Two former Padres, Tony Gwynn and Trevor Hoffman, have statues at the ballpark honoring their careers. Many believe Tatís will be the third player to earn a statue at Petco Park.

The Padres signed Tatís to a 14-year, $340-million contract before he had even played a complete season in the major leagues. If he turns out to be a superstar, it will be a great contract for the team. But what if Tatís doesn't reach superstar level? He has already been on the injured list many times in his young career. Will Tatís become one of the greatest shortstops to ever play the game? It is too early to tell, but he is definitely one of the most exciting players in the game today!

>>> Tatís fields a ball at a Padres game.

# TIMELINE

**1999** Fernando Tatís Jr. is born in San Pedro de Macoris, Dominican Republic, on January 2.

**2015** Tatís is signed by the Chicago White Sox to his first professional contract.

**2016** The White Sox trade Tatís to the San Diego Padres.

**2018** Tatís is named to the Texas League All-Star Game as a member of the San Antonio Missions.

**2019** Tatís plays in his first major league game on March 28.

**2019** On April 1, Tatís hits his first major league home run.

**2020** Tatís hits two home runs in Game 2 of the National League Wild Card Series.

**2021** The Padres sign Tatís to a 14-year, $340-million contract.

# GLOSSARY

**COVID-19** (KOH-vid nine-TEEN)—a very contagious and sometimes deadly virus that spread worldwide in 2020

**DEBUT** (DAY-byoo)—a player's first game

**ELITE** (ih-LEET)—players who are among the best in the league

**GRAND SLAM** (GRAND SLAM)—a home run with the bases loaded

**PLAYOFFS** (PLAY-awfs)—a series of games played after the regular season to decide a championship

**PROSPECT** (PROS-pekt)—a person with a bright future

**SIGNING BONUS** (SINE-ing BOH-nuhss)—a big, one-time payment a player gets when signing a contract

**SWEPT** (SWEPT)—to win a series without any losses

# READ MORE

Chandler, Matt. *Baseball's Greatest Walk-Offs and Other Crunch-Time Heroics.* North Mankato, MN: Capstone, 2020.

Rajczak, Michael. *The Greatest Baseball Players of All Time.* New York: Gareth Stevens Publishing, 2020.

Seidel, Jeff. *Pro Baseball Upsets.* Minneapolis: Lerner, 2020.

# INTERNET SITES

*ESPN: Fernando Tatis Jr.*
espn.com/mlb/player/_/id/35983/fernando-tatis-jr

*MLB: Fernando Tatís Jr. #23*
mlb.com/player/fernando-tatis-jr-665487

*National Baseball Hall of Fame*
baseballhall.org

# INDEX

# AUTHOR BIO

Matt Chandler is the author of more than 60 books for children and thousands of articles published in newspapers and magazines. He writes mostly nonfiction books with a focus on sports, ghosts and haunted places, and graphic novels. Matt lives in New York.